★ It's My State! ★ ★ ★ ★ ★

WISCONSIN
The Badger State

Margaret Dornfeld and Richard Hantula

Cavendish
Square

New York

Published in 2015 by Cavendish Square Publishing, LLC
243 5th Avenue, Suite 136, New York, NY 10016

Third Edition

Library of Congress Cataloging-in-Publication Data

Dornfeld, Margaret.
Wisconsin / Margaret Dornfeld, Richard Hantula. – [Third edition].
pages cm. — (It's my state!)
ISBN 978-1-62712-760-8 (hardcover) ISBN 978-1-62712-762-2 (ebook)
1. Wisconsin—Juvenile literature. I. Hantula, Richard. II. Title.

F581.3.D67 2014
977.5—dc23

2014015836

Editorial Director: Dean Miller
Editor, Third Edition: Nicole Sothard
Art Director: Jeffrey Talbot
Series Designer, Third Edition: Jeffrey Talbot
Layout Design, Third Edition: Erica Clendening
Production Manager: Jennifer Ryder-Talbot

The photographs in this book are used by permission and through the courtesy of: Cover Richard Price/Photographer's Choice/Getty Images; pp. 4 (top), 4 (middle), 5 (top), 5 (bottom), 8, 11 (top), 11 (bottom), 12, 14 (top), 14 (bottom), 15 (bottom), 16, 18, 20 (top), 20 (middle), 20 (bottom), 21 (top), 21 (middle), 21 (bottom), 34 (top), 34 (middle), 34 (bottom), 35 (middle), 35 (bottom), 48 (top), 48 (middle), 49 (top), 55, 64 (top), 64 (middle), 64 (bottom), 65 (top), 65 (middle), 65 (bottom), 66, 71, 75 (top), 75 (middle), 75 (bottom) Shutterstock.com; p. 4 (bottom) Bruce Marlin, via Wikimedia Commons; p. 5 (middle) © crisod/iStockPhoto.com; p. 6 Education Images/UIG/Getty Images; p. 9 David R. Frazier Photolibrary, Inc/Alamy; p. 13 J. McCormick/Shutterstock.com; p. 14 (middle) KarSol/Shutterstock.com; p. 15 (top) Wikimedia Commons; p. 15 (middle) fototehnik/Shutterstock.com; p. 17 Michael S. Quinton/National Geographic/Getty Images; p. 19 PhotoStockFile/Alamy; pp. 22, 24, 28 © North Wind Picture Archives / Alamy; pp. 27, 29, 38, 42 (top), 42 (bottom), 43 (top), 46, 54, 58 (top), 58 (bottom), 68 Getty Images; p. 31 Image ID 3728/Wisconsin Historical Society; p. 32 Image ID 8156/Wisconsin Historical Society; p. 33 Image ID 16249/Wisconsin Historical Society; p. 35 (top) © Sirimo/iStockPhoto.com; p. 36 Image ID 25167/Wisconsin Historical Society; p. 40 Sarah Hadley/Alamy; p. 41 Steve Skjold/Alamy; p. 42 (middle) Action Sports Photography/Shutterstock.com; p. 43 (middle) LC-USZ62-119765/Library of Congress, via Wikimedia Commons; p. 43 (bottom) Bettmann/Corbis; p. 45 Darren Hauck/AP Images; p. 48 (bottom) Keith Bell/Shutterstock; p. 49 (middle) © sauletas/iStockPhoto.com; p. 49 (bottom) © 2005 Sulfur, via Wikimedia Commons; pp. 50, 63 © YinYang/iStockPhoto.com; p. 52 Claver Carroll/Getty Images; p. 53 © benkrut/iStockPhoto.com; p. 56 © Squaredpixels/iStockPhoto.com; p. 57 David Nevala Photography/Getty Images; p. 58 (middle) Voces de la Frontera, via Wikimedia Commons; p. 59 © LifesizeImages/iStockPhoto.com; p. 60 John Coletti/Getty Images; p. 62 Scott Olsen/Getty Images; p. 67 GlowImages/Alamy; p. 69 Andre Jenny/Alamy; p. 70 Morry Gash/AP Images; p. 72 PHOTOTAKE Inc/Alamy; p. 73 Saxon Holt/Alamy.

Printed in the United States of America

WISCONSIN
CONTENTS

★ State Flower: Wood Violet

Wisconsin schoolchildren chose the wood violet as the state flower in 1909. The state **legislature** made it official in 1949. The wood violet has delicate purple petals. It blooms throughout the woods from March to June.

★ State Bird: Robin

A familiar sight in backyards, parks, and open farmland across the country, the robin is a symbol of spring. Robins sometimes nest on windowsills. They lay eggs that are a beautiful shade of blue.

★ State Tree: Sugar Maple

Sugar maples turn blazing gold and amber each fall. They are bursting with sap by springtime. In *Little House in the Big Woods*, author Laura Ingalls Wilder writes about her pioneer family in Wisconsin. They drilled holes in their maple trees to collect sap for making syrup.

WISCONSIN

POPULATION: 5,686,986

State Animal: Badger

The badger became Wisconsin's state animal in 1957, long after the state got its nickname. People rarely see badgers because they hunt at night. When cornered, they are tough fighters, which makes them a favorite mascot for Wisconsin sports teams.

State Fish: Muskellunge

The muskellunge, or muskie, is a large, torpedo-shaped fish known for its fighting power. The largest muskie ever caught in Wisconsin waters weighed almost 70 pounds (32 kg).

State Beverage: Milk

The state's dairy cows produce about 10 gallons (38 l) of milk a week per resident. Fortunately, Wisconsin citizens do not have to drink it all. Producers use about 90 percent of the milk to make cheese.

Dairy farms are common throughout
Wisconsin.

The Badger State

Many people picture simple farms when they think of Wisconsin. But it is a fair-sized place with a lot of variety. It has 72 counties and covers a land area of 54,310 square miles (140,663 square km). Just as common as farms are woods, marshes, high cliffs, and deep ravines. Some areas are crowded with towns and cities.

Wisconsin is a great place for people who like to hunt, camp, fish, and enjoy the great outdoors. There is also plenty to eat and drink in Wisconsin. It is a popular destination for cheese- and beer-lovers. Families enjoy places like Wisconsin Dells and Lake Geneva.

Wisconsin has so many faces that you need time to get to know it. One way to start is to look at the landscape.

Eastern Farmlands

Many people live in the eastern part of the state. Rich soil and long, mild summers started bringing farmers to this area in the nineteenth century. Wisconsin's biggest city, Milwaukee, sits on the shore of Lake Michigan. To the west is Kettle Moraine, a string of rolling hills with small lakes and marshes tucked in between.

Ice and snow pile up on the shoreline of Lake Michigan at Peninsula State Park.

Wisconsin Borders

North:	Michigan
	Lake Superior
South:	Illinois
East:	Lake Michigan
West:	Minnesota
	Iowa

The Door Peninsula in northeastern Wisconsin is a thin strip of land that reaches north into Lake Michigan. Beginning in the 1800s, farmers from Belgium, Norway, and Sweden moved there. Steep bluffs, sandy beaches, and cherry and apple orchards make up this narrow peninsula. Beyond its tip lies Washington Island, which many families from Iceland have made their home. Door County is known for its quiet, beautiful farmland, but its nickname tells of danger. High winds and churning waters near the entrance to Green Bay are so strong, early sailors called the area Death's Door.

Small towns dot the Fox River Valley, stretching from the middle of southern Wisconsin to the eastern town of Green Bay. Some of the state's most important mills and factories are here. The Fox flows into Lake Winnebago, the largest lake in the state, and then proceeds on to Green Bay. The world's first **hydropower** plant, which makes electricity from the energy of moving water, opened in 1882 on the Fox River near Appleton.

The Northwoods

Most of northern Wisconsin is covered with forests. Leafy trees such as maple, birch, oak, and aspen mix with evergreens such as spruce and pine. Tiny lakes are tucked in the miles of trees like hidden jewels. The Gogebic Range, extending from near Ashland into Michigan, was an important iron-mining area in the late nineteenth century and much of the twentieth century.

Ripe cherries hang from trees in Wisconsin's Door County.

WISCONSIN
COUNTY MAP

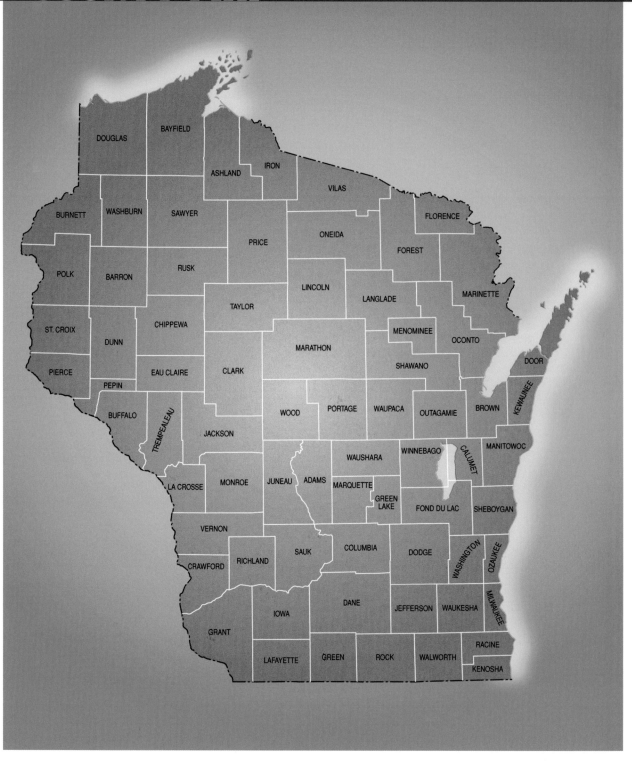

WISCONSIN
POPULATION BY COUNTY

County	Population	County	Population	County	Population
Adams County	20,875	Lafayette County	16,836	Walworth County	102,228
Ashland County	16,157	Langlade County	19,977	Washburn County	15,911
Barron County	45,870	Lincoln County	28,743	Washington County	131,887
Bayfield County	15,014	Manitowoc County	81,442	Waukesha County	389,891
Brown County	248,007	Marathon County	134,063	Waupaca County	52,410
Buffalo County	13,587	Marinette County	41,749	Waushara County	24,496
Burnett County	15,457	Marquette County	15,404	Winnebago County	166,994
Calumet County	48,971	Menominee County	4,232	Wood County	74,749
Chippewa County	62,415	Milwaukee County	947,735		
Clark County	34,690	Monroe County	44,673		
Columbia County	56,833	Oconto County	37,660		
Crawford County	16,644	Oneida County	35,998		
Dane County	488,073	Outagamie County	176,695		
Dodge County	88,759	Ozaukee County	86,395		
Door County	27,785	Pepin County	7,469		
Douglas County	44,159	Pierce County	41,019		
Dunn County	43,857	Polk County	44,205		
Eau Claire County	98,736	Portage County	70,019		
Florence County	4,423	Price County	14,159		
Fond du Lac County	101,633	Racine County	195,408		
Forest County	9,304	Richland County	18,021		
Grant County	51,208	Rock County	160,331		
Green County	36,842	Rusk County	14,755		
Green Lake County	19,051	St. Croix County	84,345		
Iowa County	23,687	Sauk County	61,976		
Iron County	5,916	Sawyer County	16,557		
Jackson County	20,449	Shawano County	41,949		
Jefferson County	83,686	Sheboygan County	115,507		
Juneau County	26,664	Taylor County	20,689		
Kenosha County	166,426	Trempealeau County	28,816		
Kewaunee County	20,574	Vernon County	29,773		
La Crosse County	114,638	Vilas County	21,430		

Source: U.S. Bureau of the Census, 2010

Dane County

Milwaukee County

During the winter, the Apostle Islands sea caves on the shores of Lake Superior are covered with ice and snow.

In the far north, hundreds of streams flow from the woods into Lake Superior. This area is known for its rust-colored rocks and tumbling waterfalls. Lake waters have hollowed out caves along their rocky shores.

Wisconsin does not have truly high mountains. Its highest point is Timms Hill in Price County in the Northwoods. Timms rises 1,952 feet (595 m) above sea level. Most of the state's big rivers, including the Wisconsin, Flambeau, Chippewa, and St. Croix, start in the Northwoods and flow southwest toward the Mississippi River. The St. Croix River and the Namekagon River, which flows into it, make up the Saint Croix National Scenic Riverway, totaling 252 miles (406 km) in length.

The Driftless Area and Central Sands

During the Ice Age that ended more than 10,000 years ago, moving slabs of ice called glaciers covered much of North America. They dragged along sand and dirt, leaving behind smooth hills and ridges called glacial drift. Kettle Moraine is an example. But the glaciers never reached the southwestern part of the state. Some of Wisconsin's most dramatic scenery is in these highlands, known as the Driftless Area.

Tall buttes (mountains or hills with steep sides and flat tops) and sandstone towers seem to rise out of nowhere in the Driftless Area. A patchwork of woods and tidy farms covers its rounded hills and narrow valleys. At the Mississippi, the land suddenly plunges. The view of the mighty river from the cliffs high above can take your breath away.

In the center of the state is a swampy plain called the Central Sands. The Wisconsin River cuts through this land, shaping a narrow canyon more than 5 miles (8 km) long called the Wisconsin Dells. The river winds between rock walls that reach 100 feet (30 m) high. The water has worn them down, creating strange and beautiful forms.

The Mississippi River flows through Wisconsin's Driftless Area.

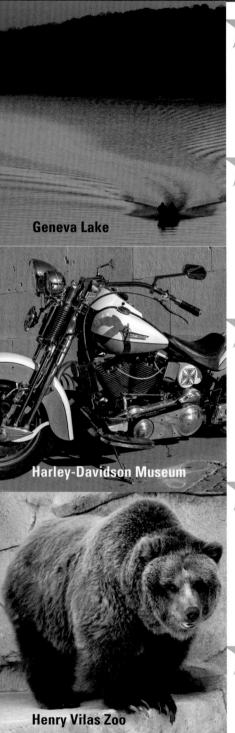

Geneva Lake

Harley-Davidson Museum

Henry Vilas Zoo

1. Big Bay State Park

Big Bay State Park is a 2,350-acre (951-ha) park on Madeline Island, the largest of 22 Apostle Islands on Lake Superior. The park has a 1.5-mile (2.4-km) beach, a campground, picnic areas, and hiking trails.

2. Cave of the Mounds

Cave of the Mounds is a natural limestone cave in southern Wisconsin. It is named after the Blue Mounds, two large, nearby hills. Cave of the Mounds lies under the southern slope of the East Mound. Visitors have been visiting the cave since its opening in 1940.

3. Geneva Lake

Geneva Lake is an 8.6-square mile (22.2-sq km) freshwater lake in southeastern Wisconsin. Visitors and residents enjoy fishing, swimming, and boating during the warm months. In the winter, the lake is good for ice fishing, snowmobiling, and skiing.

4. Harley-Davidson Museum

The Harley-Davidson Museum, in Milwaukee, is a 130,000-square foot (12,077-sq m) museum that contains more than 450 Harley-Davidson motorcycles and hundreds of thousands of artifacts. Around 300,000 people visit the museum each year.

5. Henry Vilas Zoo

This 28-acre (11-ha) zoo in Madison is a public zoo that features many different animals, including red pandas, alligators, frogs, kangaroos, and giraffes. More than 750,000 people visit this free zoo every year.

WISCONSIN

6. House on the Rock

The House on the Rock is a collection of unique rooms, streets, gardens, and shops designed by Alex Jordan, Jr. It is located north of Dodgeville, and is a regional tourist attraction.

7. Milwaukee Art Museum

The Milwaukee Art Museum, located on Lake Michigan, houses a collection of over 30,000 works of art. The museum also offers classes, tours, and events. More than 400,000 people visit each year.

8. Milwaukee Public Museum

The Milwaukee Public Museum is a natural and human history museum located in downtown Milwaukee. It has three floors of exhibits and the first IMAX Theater in the state. Visitors can see 4.5 million specimens, including animal dioramas, insects, and artifacts.

9. Noah's Ark Waterpark

Noah's Ark is a 70-acre (28-ha) water park in Wisconsin Dells. The park features waterslides, wave pools, endless rivers, bumper boats, and many other attractions. There are also arcade games and a theater.

10. Olbrich Botanical Gardens

Olbrich Botanical Gardens, in Madison, is made up of several gardens. The Sunken Garden is a traditional English garden. The Thai Garden has a tropical appearance. A Rock Garden has mostly conifers and alpine plants. There is also a meadow, and herb and rose gardens.

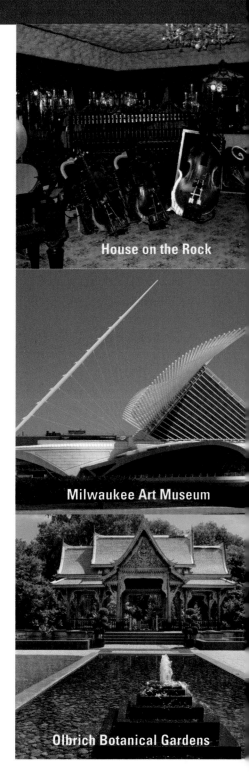

House on the Rock

Milwaukee Art Museum

Olbrich Botanical Gardens

Children play outside in the snow in Wisconsin.

Apostles and Lighthouses

At the northern tip of Wisconsin lie the Apostle Islands. Along with the neighboring mainland shore, they make up the Apostle Islands National Lakeshore. This picturesque park has more lighthouses than any other U.S. national park.

Wisconsin Weather

Wisconsin has very cold winters. In early December, temperatures may dive below 0 degrees Fahrenheit (–18 degrees Celsius) in the north. Lakes freeze over, wind whips the trees, and howling blizzards along the Gogebic Range can bring 3 feet (1 m) of snow. In northern Wisconsin, the wind, snow, sleet, and hail might last until May. But for most of the state, winter is not as harsh. For many, the winter weather is perfect for ice skating, skiing, and snowshoeing.

In the spring, tender buds grow on the tips of branches. As summer approaches, apple and cherry trees burst into bloom.

By July, the days are hot and muggy, but thunderstorms sometimes cool the afternoons. Some years, the state gets heavy rains that set off dangerous flooding. In 2007 and 2008, southern Wisconsin suffered record flooding, causing hundreds of millions of dollars in damage to homes and businesses. Wisconsin also experiences tornadoes, usually in the summer. The state averages about 21 a year. But 2005 set a record with 62 twisters. On August 18 of that year, 27 tornadoes hit the state, a record for one day.

In the cool, crisp fall, Wisconsin's woods turn flaming red, gold, and amber. But fierce storms often batter Lake Michigan in November. The winter chill sets in again as hard rain and giant waves beat the shore.

Life in the Wild

The heavy snow and rain that fall on Wisconsin help all kinds of wild plants grow. Ferns, mosses, and delicate wildflowers such as violets, trillium, and bloodroot decorate the Northwoods. Lacy morel mushrooms pop up from the ground each spring. Wild blueberries, thimbleberries, and black currants ripen each summer.

Many different kinds of orchids grow in Wisconsin. Some, such as the prairie white-fringed orchid, are very rare. Other flowers, such as the bluestem and blazing star, take root in the prairies near the Mississippi River. Marsh marigolds and swamp buttercups grow in wetlands. Clinging to the windswept sand dunes of Door Peninsula in the northeast are such hard-to-find flowers as dwarf lake iris and dune goldenrod.

Wisconsin's many plants provide food for wildlife such as white-tailed deer, black bears, beavers, porcupines, woodchucks, raccoons, and snowshoe hares. Flying squirrels

The snowshoe hare's coat changes from brownish in summer to pure white in winter.

Conservationists have worked hard to bring back gray wolves in Wisconsin.

nibble on nuts and seeds, such as beechnuts, as they glide from tree to tree. But like many other woodland animals, they come out of their nests only at night, so they are rarely seen.

The fox and the bobcat are among Wisconsin's most common predators. The gray wolf nearly disappeared from the state, but **conservationists** moved wolves to Wisconsin from other places. Now more than 600 roam the Northwoods. In 2013, it was proposed that the gray wolf be taken off the list of threatened and **endangered** species.

The lakes and rivers of the Badger State are teeming with fish such as trout, pike, perch, bass, and walleye. But the king of Wisconsin waters is the muskellunge, or muskie. This sleek, strong swimmer can grow 4 feet (1.2 m) long. It has big sharp teeth and will attack a muskrat if given the opportunity.

Wisconsin has more than 300 types of birds, from hawks, owls, and eagles to songbirds such as blackbirds, finches, and warblers. The ever-present mourning dove is the state symbol of peace. Many waterbirds migrate back and forth along the Mississippi River. Wisconsin's Horicon Marsh echoes with the cries of these ducks, geese, swans, cranes, and herons as they stop for food along the way. Most of the marsh makes up the Horicon

National Wildlife Refuge, and the rest of it is a state wildlife area.

The rare and beautiful whooping crane has not always lived in Wisconsin, but it is finding a home there now. Just a few hundred whooping cranes live in the wild. Most belong to a single flock that **migrates** between Texas and Canada. If food runs short or a disease spreads, all of the flock's birds could die. So to keep whooping cranes from dying out, **biologists** have helped to create a new flock that flies between Wisconsin and Florida.

In the summer of 2001, the scientists brought whooping crane eggs to the Necedah National Wildlife Refuge and raised the chicks themselves. They even dressed up in whooping crane costumes so the chicks would not be afraid. Cranes learn how to migrate by following their parents—so when fall came, the scientists led the way! By flying ahead of the flock in special lightweight airplanes, they got seven cranes to travel the 1,250 miles (2,000 km) to Florida. They repeated the process with more cranes in following years. Once the young cranes have made the trip south, they return north in the spring on their own. If all goes well, Wisconsin will have 125 whooping cranes by 2020.

A flock of endangered whooping cranes follows a special lightweight aircraft south for the winter. Scientists have been creative in their efforts to protect these Wisconsin birds.

10 KEY PLANTS AND ANIMALS

Dragonfly

Morel Mushroom

Red-Winged Blackbird

1. State Animal: Badger

A badger is a mammal that has a short, fat body and short legs. It has brown or black fur with white stripes on its cheeks and a stripe running from its nose to its head. Badgers live in fields, farmland, and along the edges of woods.

2. Dragonfly

Dragonflies live near bodies of water in Wisconsin. Door County is one of the few places in the United States where you'll find the Hine's emerald dragonfly, an insect as long as 3 inches (8 cm) that has shimmering green eyes. These dragonflies are endangered, which means there are so few of them, there is a risk they will die out.

3. Morel Mushroom

Many people prize morel mushrooms, often found at the base of dead trees, for their delicious flavor. But be careful—only people who know how to recognize the cone-shaped morels should collect and eat them. Other types of mushrooms can be poisonous.

4. Red-Winged Blackbird

Red-winged blackbirds nest in marshy areas of Wisconsin in early spring. They like to rest on cattails and defend their territory with their loud, long call, "ok-a-LEEEE."

5. State Bird: Robin

American Robins are gray-brown birds with warm orange-red undersides and dark heads. Common throughout North America, they are often seen on lawns searching for earthworms.

6. **State Tree: Sugar Maple**

The sugar maple became Wisconsin's State Tree in 1949. These trees can live for 300 to 400 years. Sap from the sugar maple is used for maple syrup production, and its wood is used for construction and heating homes.

7. **Trillium**

Trillium is easy to spot on the forest floor each spring. Its three large petals can be be white, purple, or pink.

8. **White-Tailed Deer**

White-tailed deer are common in wooded areas all over Wisconsin. They nibble young leaves, acorns, berries, and grass as well as wheat and alfalfa crops. Wisconsin has named the white-tailed deer the state wildlife animal.

9. **State Flower: Wood Violet**

This small flower is commonly seen in wet woodland areas, meadows, and along the road. Its leaves, which contain vitamins A and C, have been used in salads, candies, and jellies.

10. **Yellow Perch**

Schools of yellow perch swim in Lake Michigan and the large lakes and rivers of inland Wisconsin. In the 1990s, the perch population in Lake Michigan began dropping rapidly, and restrictions were imposed on yellow perch fishing. Several years later there were signs the population might be increasing again.

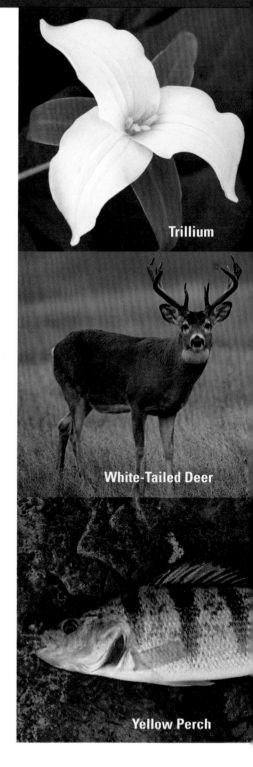

Trillium

White-Tailed Deer

Yellow Perch

From the Beginning

Here and there in southern Wisconsin, mysterious mounds can be seen. The people who made them are called Mound Builders. They began living in what is now Wisconsin more than 2,500 years ago. When seen from above, some of these mounds are long and straight. Others are shaped like animals—such as eagles, rabbits, bears, and buffalo—or people. Scholars believe that the mounds might have had some sort of religious or ceremonial purpose. Human life in present-day Wisconsin goes back even farther. Stone tools found buried in the ground show that people were around as early as 10,000 BCE.

Many groups of people have lived in the region since the days of the Mound Builders. The Menominee and Ojibwe, or Chippewa, Native Americans gathered wild rice in the north. The Ho-Chunk, or Winnebago, people settled in the central region and the south. They raised corn, beans, and squash and speared fish in rivers and streams. The Lakota also tribe lived in what is now Wisconsin. The forests were home to the Fox, or Meskwaki, the Sauk, the Potawatami, and the Kickapoo people.

Father Jacques Marquette explores the upper Mississippi River in Wisconsin.

French explorer Jean Nicolet landed on the shore of Lake Michigan in present-day Wisconsin in 1634.

The French Arrive

French explorer Étienne Brûlé visited the area around Lake Superior in 1622 or 1623. It is not clear whether he was the first European in what is now Wisconsin. Another French explorer, Jean Nicolet, is known to have visited present-day Wisconsin in 1634. He was looking for a way to sail across North America to China so the French could buy silk there and ship it home. Nicolet landed on the shore of Green Bay, where he met a group of Native Americans. "He wore a grand robe of China damask, all strewn with flowers and birds of many colors," wrote a man who knew him. Nicolet was far from China, but the Wisconsin woods held their own riches.

The forests were full of muskrats, foxes, mink, and beavers, which Europeans valued for their furs. French fur traders soon made their way to Wisconsin. Native American hunters traded their many animal skins for guns, cloth, and metal tools.

In 1673, two French explorers—Father Jacques Marquette (a Catholic priest) and Louis Jolliet (a fur trader)—became the first Europeans to cross present-day Wisconsin. They canoed from Green Bay as far as they could up the Fox River. Then, Native Americans told them where to carry their boats from the Fox to the Wisconsin River, just 1.5 miles (2.4 km) away. From there they could travel downstream to the Mississippi River. French fur traders later used this path between rivers to move between trading posts on the Great Lakes and the Mississippi.

Badgers and Lead

Many settlers mined lead in the Driftless Area in the 1820s to early 1860s. The early miners were called badgers because the tunnels they dug looked like badger holes. Wisconsin is still known as the Badger State.

Native American Wars

Between 1754 and 1763, France and Britain fought for control of eastern North America in the French and Indian War. At the end of the war, the victorious British took control of land that included what is now Wisconsin. Twenty years later, the United States won independence from Britain in the American Revolution, and Wisconsin became U.S. land.

By the early 1800s, the fur trade was fading, and settlers now wanted to move onto the Native American lands. The U.S. government talked the region's Native Americans into giving up their territory. In most cases, the natives signed official agreements called treaties with the United States. Some agreed to move west across the Mississippi River. Later on, they longed to return to their homelands.

The Black Hawk War took place in 1832 after a Sauk leader named Black Hawk helped a group of Native Americans return to their lands in Illinois. When U.S. troops came to remove them, the Native Americans fled north to Wisconsin. Black Hawk's people fought to defend themselves, but they were outnumbered. When they tried to get back over the Mississippi River, U.S. soldiers stopped them, killing many in the process.

The government let some tribes try to make a living on reservations—areas of land set aside for them. Many tribes adapted to the changing ways. Others lived in poverty among the white people, often moving from place to place in search of work and food.

The Native People

Indigenous people arrived in Wisconsin about 10,000 years ago and populated the entire region. The tribes living in the region when French fur traders arrived in 1634 were the Dakota Sioux in the western part of the state, the Ho-Chunk (Winnebago) in the southeast, the Menominee in the northeast, and the Ojibwe and Potawatomi in the northwest.

The Dakota Sioux are related to the Great Plains tribes, and the rest of the original Wisconsin tribes were part of the Eastern Woodlands group. For most Wisconsin-based Natives, the women dressed themselves in leather skirts or dresses and the men in leggings, with both genders wearing moccasins made from animal hides and beautifully decorated with beads. They created dugout or birch bark canoes, and were skilled storytellers. The tribes of the woodland group lived in rectangular houses or wigwams shingled with birch bark. The men in these tribes hunted and fished, while the women farmed and gathered food.

In the 150 years after contact was made with Europeans, the tribes of Wisconsin assisted in the fur trade. Western expansion drove the Cheyenne, Huron, Illini, Munsee, Stockbridge, and the Oneida into the state. The Stockbridge and the Oneida were sent to Wisconsin as part of an 1822 treaty negotiated with the Ho-Chunk and the Menominee. When settlers reached Wisconsin, many Natives currently living on the land were driven farther west.

The Native American population in the state has been increasing since 2000. There are now more than 50,000 indigenous people there. There are eleven federally recognized tribes and eleven reservations spread throughout the northern half of the state, including Bad River Band of Lake Superior Chippewa, Ho-Chunk Nation, Lac Courte Oreilles Band of Lake Superior Chippewa, Lac du Flambeau Band of Lake Superior Chippewa, Menominee Tribe of Wisconsin, Oneida Nation, Forest County Potawatomi, Red Cliff Band of Lake Superior Chippewa, St. Croix Chippewa, Sokaogon Chippewa (Mole Lake), and Stockbridge-Munsee.

Spotlight on the Sioux

The Sioux, also called the Dakota and the Lakota, were a Native American tribe that lived in what is now Wisconsin.

"Sioux" means "little snake," a name given to the tribe by the Chippewa (Ojibwe) Native Americans. The Sioux were nomadic, which means they never stayed in one place

This illustration depicts members of the Sioux tribe in their village.

for a very long time. They generally followed the pattern of the buffalo, or bison, which assured them that there would be food and clothing wherever they traveled.

Homes: The tribe lived in teepees (or tipis). They were made from long wooden poles, and they were covered with bison hides. The poles were tied together at the top and spread wide at the bottom to make a cone shape. Teepees could be taken down and set up quickly.

Art: Sioux men made paintings made from Buffalo-hide that were quite detailed. Women were known for their bead art, often in the form of jewelry and embroidery. They were also skilled at pottery.

Bison: The bison was the most important aspect of Sioux life. After a hunt, the tribe used the meat for food, but they also used the entire animal. The Sioux used the skin and fur to make blankets and clothes. They used the hides to make coverings for their teepees. The Sioux used the bones to make tools. Hair was used to make ropes, and the animal's tendons could be used for sewing thread and bow strings.

Powwows: The Sioux were known for their powwows. These were ceremonies that featured dancing, singing, and food.

Fur trading was an important business during the 1800s. This illustration shows the American Fur Company's trading post in Wisconsin.

Nineteenth-Century Growth

Little by little, settlers spread across the Wisconsin frontier. Many came from the East Coast, others from nearby states and territories. Some men mined lead in the southwest. Others built farms near the rivers that flowed into Green Bay. As more settlers arrived in the area, outposts such as Fort Winnebago, built in 1827, were established to make life safer for the settlers.

Wisconsin was once part of the Northwest Territory of the United States, then, in turn, the Indiana Territory, the Illinois Territory, and the Michigan Territory. In 1836, it became a territory of its own. To become a state, it needed to have at least 60,000 residents. By 1845, its population reached 155,000, but statehood also required the adoption of a constitution. In March 1848, Wisconsin voters finally approved a constitution, and two months later Wisconsin became the thirtieth state.

In the 1850s, word quickly spread that land in Wisconsin was rich and cheap. People rushed in from other parts of the country as well as from Germany, Ireland, Great Britain, Norway, Holland, Switzerland, and Belgium. Loggers cut pine from the forests and sent it down the rivers to busy sawmills. Settlers planted wheat in cleared fields. Railroads soon crisscrossed the state.

Between 1850 and 1900, Wisconsin's population swelled from about 300,000 to more than 2 million. More than 90,000 Wisconsinites took part in the Civil War from 1861 to 1865. Overall, during the second half of the nineteenth century, new industries created plenty of jobs. Factory workers made bricks, paper, machinery, and iron tools. In Milwaukee, hundreds of men and women worked in breweries. Quarrying—taking stone from the ground for use in making such things as roads and buildings—became a big industry. Today, red granite, which is quarried in Wisconsin, is the state rock.

Lumbering was a key industry, especially in the northern half of Wisconsin in the 1870s through the 1890s. Between 1888 and 1893, one-fourth of Wisconsinites' wages came from lumbering. Agriculture and the timber industry have contributed so much to the state that Wisconsin even has an official state soil, selected in 1983. Antigo silt loam is named after the Wisconsin city of Antigo. Dairy farms also spread across the state, making Wisconsin an important center for milk, butter, and cheese production.

Two train engineers pose on their steam locomotive of the Chicago, Milwaukee, St. Paul, and Pacific Railroad, which was built in the mid-1800s.

Making a Rockin' Robin

The robin is Wisconsin's State Bird, but robins can be found in almost every state in the country. Follow these simple directions to make your own robin that rocks!

What You Need

Old cereal box

Round plate

Marker or pen

Glue

Safety scissors

Red tissue paper, torn into small pieces and crumpled up

Orange construction paper

Brown or gray construction paper

What To Do

- Turn the cereal box inside out.
- Put the plate, top faced down, on the box. Trace around the plate with a pen or marker.

- Cut out the cardboard circle and fold it in half. This is the robin's body.
- Make the robin's red breast by gluing the crumpled up red tissue paper to the bottom front of the body. Make sure to do both sides.
- Cut a triangle out of the orange construction paper for the robin's beak. Glue it above the breast on the fold.
- Cut out strips of the brown or gray and orange construction paper. Glue them to the opposite end of the body from its beak. This will be the robin's tail.
- Use a marker or pen to draw the robin's eyes.
- Once finished, give the robin a tap and watch it rock!

Despite successes, the state also faced hard times. On October 8, 1871, a terrible forest fire hit northeastern Wisconsin. High winds fanned the flames into a blazing tornado that whipped the western shore of Green Bay. A large portion of six counties burned, including the entire town of Peshtigo. More than 1,000 people were killed. The Peshtigo fire remains the most deadly forest fire in U.S. history.

The Wisconsin Idea

In the 1900s, a new kind of politics gripped Wisconsin. It was introduced when Robert M. La Follette Sr. was elected governor in 1900. La Follette pushed for laws to make politics and business more honest, earning him the nickname "Fighting Bob." His sons, Robert M. Jr. and Philip, became leading politicians, too.

The La Follettes saw education as the key to good government, and they helped make the University of Wisconsin one of the nation's top schools. Wisconsin became known as a progressive state willing to try new ideas. Its formula for success—getting experts to study state problems and offer advice—was called the Wisconsin Idea.

This illustration of the Peshtigo fire appeared in *Harper's Weekly* in 1871. Some people escaped by plunging into the river.

Wisconsin was one of the first states to support workers' rights. These female factory workers are making parts for cream separators in Milwaukee around 1918.

As part of Wisconsin's progressive spirit, mill and factory workers started calling for better treatment. They wanted an eight-hour workday. They also fought for a guaranteed minimum wage. In 1911, Wisconsin became one of the first states in the country to pass a workers' **compensation** law, granting payments to people hurt on the job. In 1911, the state set up the Wisconsin Industrial Commission, which worked to ensure safe factories.

The Wisconsin Idea helped put food on the table during the Great Depression, when large numbers of people lost their jobs. In 1932, Wisconsin started the first unemployment insurance program in the United States. It gave jobless men and women money to help them get by. The state also hired people to work on major projects, such as replanting forests and building new roads.

Wars and Civil Rights

After the United States entered World War II in 1941, industries in Wisconsin, including shipbuilding and manufacturing, provided supplies for the armed forces, just as they had during World War I. The demand for war supplies created much-needed jobs for many Wisconsinites. About 120,000 served in the military in World War I (in which the United States fought from 1917 to 1918). More than 330,000 Wisconsinites served during World War II, which ended in 1945.

After the war, large numbers of African Americans from the South moved to Wisconsin. By 1960, the state had nearly 600 percent more African Americans than in 1940. These newcomers settled mainly in Milwaukee and a few other cities. They were often not allowed to live in the same areas as white people, and their children went to separate, or segregated, schools.

The Great Depression of the 1930s was a difficult time for many American families, like this one from Madison.

★ 10 ★ KEY CITIES ★ ★ ★

Milwaukee

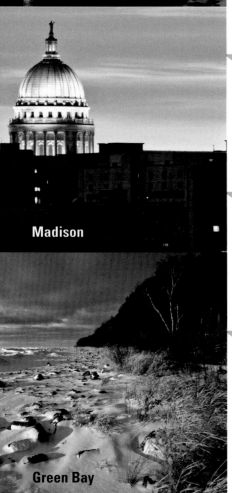

Madison

Green Bay

1. Milwaukee: population 594,833

Milwaukee is the largest city in Wisconsin. It is the main cultural and economic center of the Milwaukee–Racine–Waukesha Metropolitan Area. Residents and visitors enjoy Lake Michigan, festivals, museums, and breweries.

2. Madison: population 233,209

The state capital has a lot to offer, including extensive bike trails, museums, music festivals, and performing arts. The city has a low unemployment rate, and it is often ranked as one of the best places to live in the United States.

3. Green Bay: population 104,057

Green Bay is an industrial city, but it has plenty of things to enjoy, such as a zoo, fishing, wineries, and museums. Green Bay is best known for being the home of the NFL's Green Bay Packers. The Packers one the Super Bowl in 1997 and 2011.

4. Kenosha: population 99,218

Midway between Milwaukee and Chicago, Kenosha is known for its friendly people. The city features museums, an electric streetcar system, and the popular Kenosha HarborMarket. A Downtown district offers shopping, dining, and arts.

5. Racine: population 78,860

Racine, located on Lake Michigan, is a city with a small-town feel. Visitors can explore the nearby rural area, close-by suburbs, or the downtown area. Racine features architecture by Frank Lloyd Wright, a busy waterfront, and affordable housing.

WISCONSIN

6. Appleton: population 72,623

Appleton is one of Wisconsin's safest cities and one of the fastest growing metropolitan areas. The city has the Fox Cities Performing Arts Center, Trout Museum of Art, The Building for Kids Children's Museum, and more.

7. Waukesha: population 70,718

Waukesha was once known for its extremely clean spring water, and it was called a "spa town." Today, the city is known for its hills, forests, lakes, and rivers, and it was ranked one of the "100 Best Places to Live" by *Money* magazine in 2012.

8. Oshkosh: population 66,083

Oshkosh has a low cost of living and excellent schools. The city is the home of the EAA AirVenture Museum and the Paine Art Center and Gardens. Residents and visitors also fish, boat, and sail on nearby Lake Winnebago, Wisconsin's largest inland lake.

9. Eau Claire: population 65,883

Eau Claire, in west-central Wisconsin, was once a logging town. Today, the city offers the Paul Bunyan Museum, parades, music, and parks. There is also dining and shopping.

10. Janesville: population 63,575

Janesville is a small city located on the Rock River. It has a long history of strong industry and economic success. Janesville is known for its beautiful parks and recreational areas, including boat launches, ball fields, golf courses, and playgrounds.

Appleton

Oshkosh

Eau Claire

The U.S. Supreme Court outlawed the segregation of public schools in 1954. Cities and towns were slow to end the separation of races in public schools, however. Calls for change, giving black people the same civil rights as white people, grew louder throughout the United States.

In the 1960s, thousands of African Americans marched through the streets of Milwaukee to demand the right to live in the same areas as white residents. It was called fair, or open, housing. The state legislature passed an open-housing law in 1965, but it was rather weak. Riots in Milwaukee during the summer of 1967 left four people dead. In April 1968, the U.S. Congress enacted a fair-housing law for the entire country. Milwaukee then quickly passed its own strong fair-housing law. The federal courts also forced Milwaukee to desegregate its schools, and the city began carrying out the court order in 1979.

During the 1960s, many students on college campuses in the state, especially at the University of Wisconsin in Madison, began actively opposing the Vietnam War. (Other protests occurred on campuses nationwide.) In 1970, protesters used firebombs against a university building in Madison. Some of the antiwar protesters went on to fight for other issues, such as environmental protection laws.

Civil rights activist and Catholic priest James Groppi leads a fair housing march down a Milwaukee sidewalk in 1967.

10 KEY DATES IN STATE HISTORY

1. **c. 700 BCE**
Native Americans called Mound Builders begin living in what is now Wisconsin. Some mounds they built are long and straight, and others are shaped like animals.

2. **1634**
After landing in Green Bay, French explorer Jean Nicolet becomes the first European known to have landed in what is now Wisconsin. He comes into contact with Native Americans.

3. **1763**
After the French and Indian War, the Wisconsin region becomes British territory.

4. **September 3, 1783**
After the British are defeated in the American Revolution, the land that is now Wisconsin becomes part of the United States.

5. **1836**
After being a part of the Northwest Territory, Indiana Territory, Illinois Territory, and Michigan Territory, the land becomes the Wisconsin Territory.

6. **May 29, 1848**
After its population reaches 155,000 and its people adopt a constitution, Wisconsin becomes the thirtieth U.S. state.

7. **October 8, 1871**
A large forest fire in northeast Wisconsin spreads quickly due to high winds. More than 1,000 people die in the town of Peshtigo.

8. **July 1921**
Wisconsin passes an equal rights bill. It states that women "shall have the same rights and privileges under the law as men..."

9. **December 2, 1954**
Joseph McCarthy is blamed for unbecoming conduct by his fellow members of the U.S. Senate, thereby ending his investigation into communists in government and other institutions, also know as McCarthyism.

10. **November 4, 2008**
Wisconsin voter turnout in the U.S. presidential election (almost 73 percent) is second only to Minnesota's.

A Green Bay Packers fan cheers on the team. Packers fans are nicknamed "cheeseheads."

The People

Wisconsin's people come from many different backgrounds, and they are proud of their varied **heritage**. But the experience of living in the Badger State—braving snowstorms, working in fields or factories, listening to geese pass overhead, or watching a football game—also brings them together. In spite of their differences, Wisconsinites share many common goals and a strong sense of community.

European Roots

European families once came to Wisconsin by the thousands in search of land and political or religious freedom. Their hopes and dreams, their music and stories, help shape the state's culture today.

More than two-fifths of Wisconsin's population is at least partly of German heritage. Most German **immigrants** came to the state between 1845 and 1900. German Americans helped turn Milwaukee into America's leading beer-brewing city. Traditional German foods such as bratwurst, sauerkraut, and schaumtorte, a melt-in-your-mouth dessert often served with whipped cream and strawberries, are still popular all over the state.

Turner Hall of Monroe is a cultural center for Swiss heritage in Wisconsin.

The Polka State

The polka, brought by settlers from central Europe, is the state dance. Wisconsinites play polka music on the radio, at weddings and town festivals, and even at football games.

In Milwaukee, you will find tasty Irish stew, Italian pasta, Serbian pastries, Swiss fondue, and Polish sausages called kielbasa. European traditions are alive in other parts of the state as well. Just south of Milwaukee, in Racine, Danish bakeries make a fruit-filled coffeecake called kringle. Kewaunee County, in eastern Wisconsin, is known for its Czech and Belgian heritage, while in the north, family names are often Finnish. Farmers from Norway settled many towns in southern Wisconsin. On May 17, they celebrate Norway's independence day, dancing to music played on the Hardanger fiddle, a beautifully decorated Norwegian violin.

From Near and Far

African Americans have a long history in Wisconsin. Black fur traders worked in the area in the 1700s. In the 1800s, African Americans lived in the state's cities or built their own farming towns. In the late 1800s, the African-American community at Pleasant Ridge, near Lancaster, had its own church and school. Today, Milwaukee, Racine, and Madison have the state's largest African-American communities.

Many families have moved to the Midwestern states from Southeast Asia. These Hmong sisters watch a local parade from their steps.

John Bardeen

Matt Kenseth

Georgia O'Keeffe

1. John Bardeen

John Bardeen was born in 1908 in Madison. Bardeen received his first Nobel Prize in 1956 for helping to invent the transistor. His second, in 1972, was for his research on superconductivity, the ability of some materials to carry, or conduct, electricity without any resistance at all.

2. Belle Case La Follette

La Follette, born in Wisconsin in 1859, was the first woman to graduate from the University of Wisconsin Law School. As a respected public speaker and journalist, she worked for women's rights, opposed war, and fought for child labor reform and racial equality.

3. Harry Houdini

Ehrich Weiss was born in Budapest, Hungary, in 1874 and moved with his family to Appleton, Wisconsin, when he was four. He grew up to become one of the most amazing magicians of his time—Harry Houdini. He was best known as an escape artist.

4. Matt Kenseth

Matthew Roy "Matt" Kenseth was born in Cambridge. He is an American professional stock car racing driver in the NASCAR Sprint Cup Series, in which he has won more than 30 races as of 2014.

5. Georgia O'Keeffe

Georgia O'Keeffe was born in 1887 in Sun Prairie. She studied at the Art Institute of Chicago and later moved to New Mexico. O'Keeffe was inspired by the landscape there. She is best known for her flower canvases and landscapes.

6. Danica Patrick

Born in Beloit, Danica Patrick dropped out of high school to pursue racing. She was the fourth woman to race in the Indianapolis 500. In early 2013, Patrick won the time trials at NASCAR's Daytona 500, becoming the first woman to do so. She placed eighth in the race.

7. Les Paul

Les Paul gained fame as a guitarist, but he is remembered for helping to develop the solid-body electric guitar. Born in 1915 in Waukesha, he played the harmonica and banjo before turning to the guitar. He was admitted to the Rock and Roll Hall of Fame in 1988 and the Inventors Hall of Fame in 2005.

8. Orson Welles

Born in Kenosha in 1915, Orson Welles began his career as a stage actor before moving to radio. He later starred in films such as *The Third Man* and *Citizen Kane*, which he also co-wrote and directed. *Citizen Kane* is often called the greatest movie ever made.

9. Laura Ingalls Wilder

Laura Ingalls Wilder is the author of the *Little House* books, about life on the frontier. Born in Pepin in 1867, Wilder decided to share her story. One of her best-loved books, *Little House in the Big Woods*, takes place where she was born.

10. Frank Lloyd Wright

Frank Lloyd Wright, born in Richland Center in 1867, was known around the world for his original buildings. He was famous for combining sleek, modern shapes with light and nature.

Les Paul

Orson Welles

Laura Ingalls Wilder

Who Wisconsinites Are

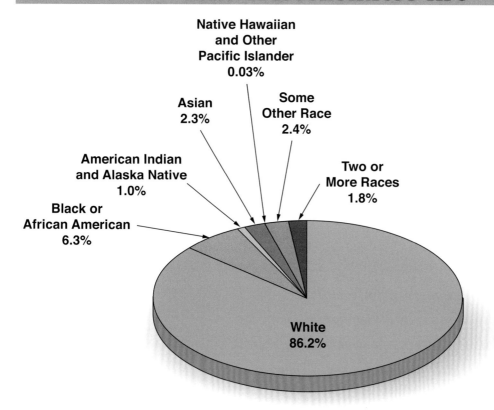

Native Hawaiian
and Other
Pacific Islander
0.03%

Asian
2.3%

Some
Other Race
2.4%

American Indian
and Alaska Native
1.0%

Two or
More Races
1.8%

Black or
African American
6.3%

White
86.2%

**Total Population
5,686,986**

Hispanic or Latino (of any race):

• 336,056 people (5.9%)

Note: The pie chart shows the racial breakdown of the state's population based on the categories used by the U.S. Bureau of the Census. The Census Bureau reports information for Hispanics or Latinos separately, since they may be of any race. Percentages in the pie chart may not add to 100 because of rounding.

Source: U.S. Bureau of the Census, 2010 Census

Many of Wisconsin's newest immigrants have come from Asia and Latin America. Members of a Southeast Asian group called the Hmong began moving to the state in the 1970s. Their language and culture are part of many communities. The town of Appleton, for example, is the home of a Hmong radio station. Wisconsin's Hispanic population, which more than doubled between 1990 and 2000, is still growing fast in cities such as Milwaukee, Madison, and Racine. By 2007, the state's Hispanic population was estimated to have grown 40 percent since 2000. Many Spanish-speaking families come from Mexico or Puerto Rico.

The people who have been in the region the longest are Native Americans. More than 54,000 Native Americans currently live in Wisconsin. Many of them call Milwaukee or Madison home, but many also return often to one of Wisconsin's eleven reservations. These lands belong to the Ojibwe, Ho-Chunk, Menominee, Oneida, Potawatomi, and Stockbridge-Munsee tribes. Throughout the year, different Native American groups hold traditional festivals and celebrations. These special events are a way to honor their past and share their cultures with others.

Taking the Lead

People have been coming to Wisconsin to start anew for hundreds of years. That might be one reason the state has a reputation for being open to new ideas. In the early 1900s, Wisconsin was one of the first states in the country to support women's rights, improvements for workers, and laws to keep big business from having too much power. In 1919, it was the first state to ratify (approve) the Nineteenth Amendment to the U.S. Constitution, giving women the right to vote. Two years later, it became the first state to pass a law giving women the same rights as men.

One issue facing citizens in Wisconsin today is the divide between black and white communities. In the Milwaukee area, for example, African Americans tend to live in the central city, while the suburbs have mostly white residents. In 2007, African-American males were nearly three times more likely to be out of work than white males in Milwaukee County. The schools in the central city are some of the state's most troubled. That may explain why only 63 percent of the state's black students compared to 92 percent of its white students graduated from high school in 2012.

A first grader learns how to read using an online program in one of Milwaukee's south side elementary schools.

Fans start to fill the stands before a Green Bay Packers game at Lambeau Field.

In Their Own Words

"Wisconsin's a special place."—Brett Favre, former quarterback for Wisconsin's Green Bay Packers

Wisconsin is focusing on education to make things more equal. In 1990, Milwaukee became the first U.S. city to start a "school choice" program. Although a number of parents believe private schools provide a better education than public schools, private school **tuition** costs too much for many families. Under the school choice program, families can get public money to send their children to private schools. The money comes in the form of a voucher—an agreement to take funds from public schools to help pay for private school educations.

At the beginning of 2014, there were 125 private schools in the program, educating more than 25,000 students. Still, not everyone thinks school choice is a good idea. Some worry that it hurts the public educational system and students. Some studies show that students in private schools do not perform any better than those in public schools. Therefore, people against the school choice program feel that there should only be public schools on which the community can focus.

Wisconsin Sports

The Badger State is big on sports. The state's Major League Baseball team, the Brewers, is based in Milwaukee. The Milwaukee Bucks represent the state in the National Basketball Association (NBA). When football season begins, nothing gets people more excited than a Green Bay Packers game. Fans will bundle up and sit through snowstorms to watch the Packers play at icy Lambeau Field.

Outdoor sports such as boating, swimming, skiing, and snowmobiling are popular in Wisconsin. Hikers can climb portions of the U.S. North Country National Scenic Trail as well as the Ice Age Trail, a national and state scenic trail in central and southern Wisconsin more than 1,000 miles (1,600 km) long.

Hunting is another popular outdoor pastime. The favorite retriever dog of many Wisconsin hunters is the American water spaniel. One of the few breeds of dogs that originated in the United States, it was developed in Wisconsin. The American water spaniel is the state dog.

With more than 15,000 lakes in the state, many people enjoy boating and fish for much of the year. Sturgeon fishing on Lake Winnebago, however, is allowed only for a short time in February. The ice at that time is usually like a layer of thick rock, and the temperature may drop to –20 °F (–29 °C). But hearty anglers say the thrill of cutting a hole in the ice and spearing one of these monsters is worth it. Sturgeon can grow 6 feet (1.8 m) long, weigh up to 80 pounds (36 kg) or more, and live as long as 150 years.

Fishing is such a big part of Wisconsin life that it can cause arguments. For example, Native Americans have the right to spear walleye and muskie on their old hunting grounds before the regular fishing seasons opens in spring. Some people claim the Native Americans take too many fish. In the past, the debate over traditional Native American spearfishing became so heated that fights sometimes broke out as protesters tried to change Wisconsin's fishing laws.

In 1983, however, the federal courts ruled that under the treaties with the U.S. government, the Ojibwe tribe had the right to early spearfishing each spring. Biologists studying Wisconsin's lakes and streams also concluded that the fish population is healthy enough for everyone to get enough fish.

Bayfield Apple Festival

Brat Days

EAA AirVenture

1. American Birkebeiner Ski Race

Thousands of athletes glide across approximately 30 miles (50 km) of snow in February at the biggest cross-country ski race in North America.

2. Bayfield Apple Festival

Each October, apple farmers near Lake Superior celebrate the harvest by serving up all kinds of apple-filled treats, from pie and dumplings to sausage. The festival also features music, artists, and vendors.

3. Brat Days

The bratwurst, or "brat," is Wisconsin's most popular sausage. This feast, usually held in late July or early August in Sheboygan, serves it any number of ways, including on pizzas or in tacos. There is also a brat-eating contest and musical entertainment.

4. Experimental Aircraft Association [EAA] AirVenture

Daredevil pilots tear up the sky at this July event that takes place in Oshkosh, where experts show off thousands of historic and modern planes. The event also features rides, food, shopping, and music.

5. Green County Cheese Days

Watch an expert make cheese in a giant copper kettle at this Swiss-American festival in Monroe, held every two years in September. Visitors to this festival also enjoy music, shopping, and all the cheese they can eat!

6. Honor the Earth Powwow

Native Americans from all around the Great Lakes region perform traditional ceremonies, songs, and dances at the Lac Courte Oreilles Ojibwe Reservation in July. More than 10,000 people from Wisconsin, Canada, and other states attend each year.

7. Lumberjack World Championship

Professional male and female lumberjacks and logrollers from around the world take part in this competition, held in July in Hayward. More than 12,000 people watch events that include speed sawing, speed climbing, logrolling, and chopping.

8. Summerfest

Big-name rock, pop, rhythm-and-blues, and country musicians perform along the shore of Lake Michigan in Milwaukee during this 11-day event beginning in late June. Summerfest is considered the world's largest music festival.

9. Warrens Cranberry Festival

Each September, tiny Warrens hosts the world's biggest cranberry festival, featuring a big marching-band parade and hundreds of arts-and-crafts, antiques, and farm-products booths.

10. Wisconsin State Fair

Champion dairy cows, carnival rides, live entertainment, and many different types of food are the focus of this August event in West Allis. There are also marching bands, demonstrations, pig races, and much more.

Lumberjack World Championship

Warrens Cranberry Festival

Wisconsin State Fair

The Wisconsin State Capitol is located in Madison.

How the Government Works

The people of Wisconsin have a say in how the state grows and changes. They help run the Badger State by voting for leaders whose ideas they believe in and by sharing their own ideas. This is true both for local government—the governments of counties, cities, villages, and towns—and for the state government.

Local Government

Each county is governed by a group, or board, of officials called supervisors, elected by the people. Most city governments are headed by an elected mayor and **council**. Other cities have a council but no mayor. Instead, the elected council chooses a manager to run the city. Most villages are headed by an elected president and board of **trustees**. Instead of a president, some villages have a manager, who is picked by the board. Areas that do not belong to a city or a village are governed by a town government. Each town is headed by an elected board of supervisors.

Another unit of government is the school district, which runs the public schools. Wisconsin has more than 426 school districts, each governed by an elected board.

Every year, each town holds a meeting, at which citizens discuss and vote on important matters. Decisions made at the meeting then guide the work of the town supervisors.

Edwin Blashfield's mural "Resources of Wisconsin" decorates the ceiling of the Wisconsin State Capitol rotunda. It is the only granite dome in the United States.

The First Kindergarten

America's first kindergarten was started in Watertown in 1856 by Margarethe Schurz. Schurz first learned the principles of kindergarten in Germany. After moving to Wisconsin, Schurz began teaching children in her home and then a local building. Before long, kindergarten became a regular part of the school curriculum, or plan.

In addition, when officials in other types of local government are making an important decision, they often hold a public meeting at which citizens can voice their opinions.

Branches of Government

Executive

The executive branch carries out the state's laws. It is headed by the governor. The governor suggests laws and starts programs that he or she thinks will benefit the state and appoints members of state boards and commissions. The governor is elected to a four-year term, as are the other chief members of the executive branch—the lieutenant governor, secretary of state, attorney general, treasurer, and state superintendent of public instruction.

Legislative

The Wisconsin legislature is divided into two houses: the Senate, with 33 members, and the assembly, with 99 members. Each senator serves a four-year term, while members of the assembly are elected for two years. The legislature develops, presents, and approves new laws.

Judicial

The highest court in Wisconsin is the state Supreme Court. Decisions made by lower courts can be appealed to the Wisconsin Supreme Court, which has seven justices, each elected to a ten-year term. Serving under the Supreme Court is the court of appeals, which mainly hears appeals from lower courts. Most cases are heard first by circuit courts. The judges of appellate and circuit courts are elected to six-year terms.

How a Bill Becomes a Law

Each member of the Wisconsin legislature represents the people of a certain district, or part of the state. Legislature members meet with citizens regularly to discuss whether to change old laws or create new laws. They write a draft, or bill, for every new law they propose.

The North Hearing Room in Wisconsin's State Capitol is used by the legislature for public committee hearings.

Governor Scott Walker signs a bill into law.

Bills can be introduced in either the Senate or the Assembly in what is called a first reading. Usually a **committee** of senators or assembly members then studies the bill. The committee may hold a public hearing so that people outside the government can say what they think of the proposal. If the bill receives support in the committee, it usually goes back to the Senate or Assembly for a second reading. Members discuss the bill's good and bad points and may change, or amend, it.

When members have voted on all the amendments, the bill gets a third reading. Then the Senate or Assembly votes on it. If a majority of members votes in favor of the bill, it passes. Then it moves to the other house, where the same steps are repeated, except that the second house may skip the committee stage. Any amendments passed by one house also have to be approved by the other house.

Once both houses accept a bill, it goes to the governor, who can either allow it to become a law or reject it. The bill becomes a law if the governor signs it or simply does not reject, or veto, it. Even if the governor vetoes the bill, it can still become law if two-thirds of the members of each house again vote in favor of it.

Issues and Laws

One issue debated by Wisconsin citizens and lawmakers in recent years is protection of the state's landscape. As towns and cities have grown larger, farmlands have disappeared. Many citizens believe that cities should control the way they grow.

A law called the Smart Growth Initiative, which was passed by the Senate and Assembly and signed by the governor in 1999, says towns must carefully plan how they use the land around them. They must also make the most of the space they already have and conserve the state's woods, marshes, fields, and farms. Critics, however, worry that the law takes away rights from property owners and lets the state control local decisions about land use. In 2005, the governor vetoed an attempt by the legislature to repeal the law.

Power lines are one of the things that towns must carefully plan under the Smart Growth Initiative.

Wisconsin Works helps people gain work experience and job skills.

Wisconsin has also debated how best to take care of people who need public assistance. In 1997, it started Wisconsin Works, a job-training and employment program for the poor. The idea behind Wisconsin Works, or W-2, is that the government should help jobless people to find work instead of just giving them money. The goal is to help citizens become independent.

When W-2 was created, it was admired so much that it became a model for a national program. The number of people getting state aid dropped by 50 percent between 1997 and 2000. But critics worried that some people might not be getting enough help from W-2. A new state agency set up in 2008—the Department of Children and Families—oversees the W-2 program to improve services for families needing assistance.

A bicyclist wears a "One Less Car" sign on his back during a demonstration at the Wisconsin State Capitol. Protecting the environment is very important to Wisconsinites.

POLITICAL FIGURES
FROM WISCONSIN

★ Tammy Baldwin: U.S. Senator, 2013–

Tammy Baldwin was born in Madison in 1962. From 1993 to 1999, Baldwin represented her state's 78th District in the Wisconsin State Assembly. She went on to become Wisconsin's first congresswoman in the U.S. House of Representatives. Then, in 2012, Baldwin became the first Wisconsin woman elected to the U.S. Senate.

★ Vel Phillips: Wisconsin Secretary of State, 1979–1983

Velvalea Rodgers "Vel" Phillips was born in Milwaukee in 1924. She became the first African-American woman to graduate from the University of Wisconsin-Madison's law school. A member of the NAACP, in 1978 Phillips was the first African-American and the first woman to be elected Secretary of State of Wisconsin.

★ Paul Ryan: U.S. House of Representatives, 1999–

Paul Ryan was born in 1970 in Janesville. Ryan became the U.S. Representative of Wisconsin's Congressional District 1 in 1999. In 2012, he was the vice-presidential running mate of Republican Mitt Romney, who lost to President Barack Obama.

WISCONSIN
YOU CAN MAKE A DIFFERENCE

Contacting Lawmakers

If you are a Wisconsinite, you can find out who your state legislators are and how to contact them. Go to:

www.legis.state.wi.us/waml

Enter your street address or the name of your city, village, or town. With that information, you can send an email or write a letter to your legislators.

Other sections of the website allow visitors to learn more about the Wisconsin state legislature and how it works, read state laws, and find various documents.

Joining the Action

If you want to support an idea you believe in, there are many ways to get involved. One step is to write a letter or send an email to a state leader. You can write to the governor, for example, or to your representatives in the legislature. Another way to make your voice heard is by joining a club or organization that supports the same causes you do. A group often has more power than an individual. When people team up, they are difficult to ignore.

It is also good to read newspapers (in print or online) and get news from the radio or television or the websites of TV news organizations, so that you can keep up-to-date on what is happening in your state. Since 2007, Wisconsinites have had an easy way to get a more complete and close-up look at their state government in action. The private network WisconsinEye, broadcasting on television and the Internet, covers proceedings in all three branches.

Wisconsin is home for thousands of dairy farmers.

Making a Living

When Europeans first came to what is now Wisconsin, they found a land full of promise. Green forests offered timber for building. The south and the west were blessed with rich soil. The region also had plenty of water, from its thousands of lakes, rivers, and streams to its major waterways—Lakes Michigan and Superior and the Mississippi River. Over the years, these natural resources have more than lived up to their powerful potential. People have used them to build booming industries that have become the backbone of Wisconsin's strong economy.

America's Dairyland

Take a drive across the southern part of the state, from Prairie du Chien to Milwaukee, and one sight will soon become familiar: black-and-white spotted cows grazing peacefully on green pastures. Wisconsin's 1.27 million dairy cows produced more than 27 billion pounds (12 billion kg) of milk in 2013. Its factories make one-fourth of the nation's cheese. Thousands of tons of dried and evaporated milk and millions of gallons of ice cream are made in the state, too. It is no wonder Wisconsin is known as America's Dairyland.

About half of Wisconsin's farm income comes from its dairy products. Another large portion is earned selling chickens, eggs, beef cattle, and hogs.

A boy milks a cow on his grandfather's farm. The family milks more than 100 dairy cattle a day.

In Their Own Words

"Conservation is a state of harmony between men and land. . . . Harmony with land is like harmony with a friend; You cannot cherish his right hand and chop off his left."—Wisconsin conservationist Aldo Leopold

Wisconsin farmers also grow corn, which is the official State Grain, as well as hay, soybeans, winter wheat, mint, and tobacco. They are among the country's top producers of vegetables for canning, including green peas, snap beans, sweet corn, and cabbage for sauerkraut.

Wisconsin leads the country in the production of cranberries, which grow in the marshy soil of the Central Sands and in several northern counties. Orchards in Door and Kewaunee counties supply the Midwest with apples and tart cherries.

Today Wisconsin has far fewer farms than it did 100 years ago, but the farms that survive are much larger. Together they cover almost half the land.

These men are harvesting cranberries in a bog near Warrens, Wisconsin.

10 KEY INDUSTRIES

Cranberries

1. Cranberries

The cranberry is the state fruit. Roughly half of the nation's cranberries are grown in Wisconsin. Wisconsin cranberry growers annually harvest enough cranberries to supply every man, woman, and child in the world with 26 cranberries.

2. Dairy

With more than 10,000 dairy farms, Wisconsin is a leading producer of milk, butter, and cheese. The largest grouping of dairy cows is in the area between Green Bay and Monroe.

3. Design and Technology

This growing industry in Wisconsin includes hardware and software development, design and communication services, mail-order houses, as well as retail stores. A young population and the state's proximity to major cities help this industry thrive.

4. Education

The University of Wisconsin system includes 13 four-year colleges and an equal number of two-year colleges. The state is also home to leading private schools, such as Marquette and Lawrence universities and Beloit College.

5. Healthcare

Healthcare-related jobs have shown steady and consistent growth in Wisconsin. The University of Wisconsin-Madison is one of the top recipients for federal research funding.

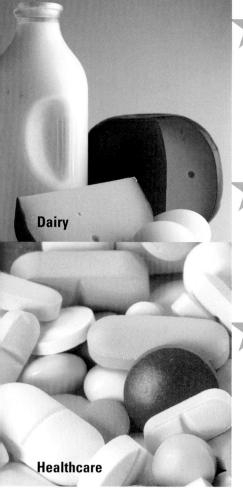

Dairy

Healthcare

WISCONSIN

 6. **Life Sciences**

Wisconsin's Madison region is a leader in **biotechnology** research and development. Many life science companies have their headquarters in the area. The industry employs more than 7,000 people.

 7. **Machinery**

The Badger State is a major producer of heavy machinery. These products include **turbines**, tractors, heating and cooling equipment, metalworking machines, and construction equipment.

 8. **Mining**

Used in the construction industry, Wisconsin's most important mined products are sand, gravel, and crushed stone. Frac sand is found in the hills and river bluffs of west-central Wisconsin. This sand is used in a special type of drilling method to find oil and natural gas.

 9. **Paper**

Wisconsin is one of the leading producers of paper in the United States. Its gigantic mills create wood pulp from trees, such as pine, poplar, spruce, and hemlock.

 **Waterways**

Wisconsin ships goods around the world from its Great Lakes ports. Its 15,000 inland lakes and more than 10,000 miles (16,000 km) of trout streams, as well as its Great Lakes shorelines, help keep its tourist industry strong as well.

Machinery

Paper

Waterways

Recipe for Macaroni and Cheese

Cheese is an important part of life in Wisconsin, and residents are very passionate about cooking with it. Use this recipe to make one of the most common and delicious cheese-related recipes: macaroni and cheese.

What You Need

½ lb (225 g) macaroni, or similar pasta

2 tbsp (30 g) butter

2 tbsp (13 g) flour

2 cups (480 ml) whole milk

½ tsp (2.5 ml) salt

½ tsp (2.5 ml) paprika

¼ tsp (2.5 ml) pepper

2 cups (180 g) Monterey Jack cheese, shredded

1 cup (90 g) shredded Cheddar Jack or Colby Jack cheese

What to Do

• Have an adult help you use the stove.

• Bring a large pot of water to boil, and cook the macaroni according to the directions on the box.

• Heat a sauce pan over medium heat. Add the butter to the pan and melt. Then add the flour.

Whisk together until the butter mixture starts to boil and foam. Then cook for another minute until it starts to turn light brown.

• Slowly mix in the whole milk. Continue to whisk and cook until it starts to thicken.

• Add the salt, pepper, paprika, and Monterey Jack cheese.

• Whisk until the cheese is fully melted.

• Pour ½ cup (45 g) of the cheese sauce into the bottom of a bowl.

• Add 1 cup (140 g) of cooked noodles to the bowl.

• Top with ½ cup (45 g) of shredded Cheddar Jack or Colby Jack cheese.

• Mix cheese sauce, macaroni, and shredded cheese together.

• Enjoy!

Manufacturing

Agriculture has always been an important part of the Wisconsin economy, but manufacturing has made the state grow and prosper. Huge paper mills near Green Bay and in the Fox River Valley produce everything from tissues to typing paper. Factories in the Milwaukee area make X-ray machines and other medical equipment, engines and turbines, power cranes, farm equipment, knives, and other metal tools.

Crazy Companies

The Tommy Bartlett Exploratory is an attraction in Wisconsin Dells that has more than 175 interactive activities that focus on science, technology, and space. The Exploratory also has a Russian Space Station MIR core module!

A foundry worker operates a metal saw in a Wisconsin factory.

A view of the Harley-Davidson plant in Menomonee Falls, Wisconsin.

One well-known Milwaukee business, the Harley-Davidson Motor Company, has been making motorcycles since 1903.

Food processing plays a major role in Wisconsin's economy, too. Creameries and cheese factories dot the state, and Lakeside Foods, one of the largest vegetable canners in the country, is based in Manitowoc. Food-processing plants in Rock County make snack foods such as potato chips and corn chips.

Given Wisconsin's strong German heritage, it is no surprise that the state is also home to a successful sausage industry.

Milwaukee has been known as the beer capital of the United States. It had almost 160 breweries by the time of the Civil War. Milwaukee was once home to the giant Schlitz, Pabst, and Miller breweries. But by 2000, only Miller remained as the city's beer powerhouse. Wisconsin today has dozens of microbreweries—companies that make gourmet beer in small batches.

Tourism

Wisconsin is one of the Midwest's most popular vacation places, and visitors spent more than $10 billion in 2012. Visitors love to fish its lakes and streams and sunbathe on the sandy beaches of Lake Michigan. In winter, thousands of miles (km) of snowmobile trails attract adventurers.

Tourists also come to see Wisconsin's unique architecture. Twentieth-century architect Frank Lloyd Wright's elegant buildings are scattered across the state. Even more spectacular is the Quadracci Pavilion of the Milwaukee Art Museum. Set on the shore of Lake Michigan, this graceful structure of steel, glass, and white concrete, designed by Spanish architect Santiago Calatrava, looks like a bird about to take flight. Completed in 2001 at a cost of more than $100 million, the pavilion is famous around the world.

The Milwaukee Art Museum addition, designed by Santiago Calatrava, features a movable, winglike sunscreen.

Milwaukee's Potawatomi Bingo Casino opened in 1991.

Wisconsin's Native American reservations and casinos are another big tourist attraction. Like most states, Wisconsin forbids gambling. But in 1988, Congress passed a law stating that such rules do not apply on Native American lands. Since then, many Wisconsin tribes have built casinos in an effort to earn money. On many reservations, more people work in gaming than in any other business, and the hotels and restaurants that surround the casinos have created even more jobs. As a result, the population on reservations is rising.

Protecting the Land

Wisconsinites want their state to have a strong economy, but not at the expense of the state's natural resources and beauty. Industries such as manufacturing, tourism, and even farming can

Wisconsinites value their state's
lakes and streams.

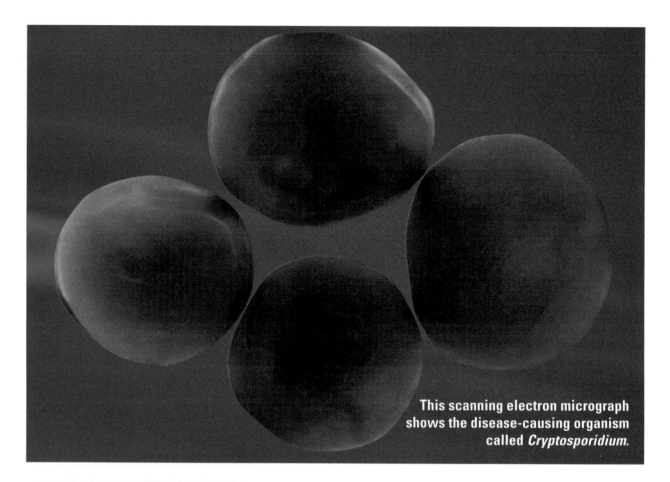

This scanning electron micrograph shows the disease-causing organism called *Cryptosporidium*.

Wisconsin Under Water

Hundreds of millions of years ago the land that is now Wisconsin lay under a warm shallow sea. Today, across the state, you can find fossils, or remains, of small creatures called trilobites, which lived in that sea. The type of trilobite called *Calymene celebra* is the state fossil.

put a heavy burden on the environment and the natural resources that keep the economy alive. A big challenge that faces the state today is protecting its most plentiful resource—water.

Water pollution has threatened Wisconsin for more than a century. Paper mills were once some of the state's worst polluters. They dumped tons of harmful chemicals into rivers and lakes, causing fish to die. In the 1960s, laws were passed that required companies to control their waste. As a result, the waters around the factories and centers of industry are much cleaner.

A bigger worry these days is a problem called nonpoint source pollution. Many of the unhealthy chemicals that find their way into Wisconsin's water do not come from a single place such as a factory.

Instead, they come from a variety of sources, such as farmers who spread **pesticides**, cars that drip motor oil, and construction workers who use tar to repair roads. As rain or melted snow flows across fields, driveways, and highways, it picks up these poisons and carries them along until they reach streams, rivers, lakes, and wetlands.

Almost half of Wisconsin's streams and 90 percent of its inland lakes are threatened by nonpoint source pollution. The results can be deadly. In 1993, a tiny organism called *Cryptosporidium* got into Milwaukee's drinking water. As a result, about 400,000 people got sick, and dozens died. Scientists think the "bug" was probably carried from fields full of cow manure.

The state now purifies, or cleans, its water more carefully. But to keep new poisons from turning up, it is focusing on prevention, too. The government is helping farmers switch to new methods that keep animal waste and chemicals from being washed away. Planting grass along waterways, for example, helps trap particles in the soil.

Wherever you live, you and your family can help by using natural fertilizers. You can keep the ground free of pet waste. You can also plant bushes, trees, and other plants to soak up the rain—such as in a well-planned rain garden.

Residents and businesses can help reduce polluted runoff from roads and roofs by planting rain gardens. Native plantings capture rainwater that filters slowly into the ground instead of running off into storm sewers.

WISCONSIN
STATE MAP

Lake Superior

Apostle Islands
National Lakeshore
Outer Island
Stockton Island

Madeline Island

Superior

2

2

53

63

Bad River
Indian
Reservation

Chequamegon
National
Forest

Turtle-Flambeau
Flowage

Northern Highland-
American Legion
State Forest

Nicolet
National
Forest

Menominee R.

Hayward

Lake
Chippewa

Lac du Flambeau
Indian Reservation

51

45

St. Croix R.

St. Croix
National
Scenic Riverway

Lac Courte
Oreilles Indian
Reservation

Flambeau R.

8

Rhinelander

8

Washington
Island

Timms Hill

Wisconsin R.

63

53

Merrill

Menominee
Indian
Reservation

141

Chambers
Island

8

Marinette

Green
Bay

Peninsula
State Park

94

Menomonie

Crystal
Cave

Chippewa Falls

Eau Claire

Wausau

Marshfield

39

45

41

Sturgeon Bay

Door
Peninsula

River Falls

10

63

53

Chippewa R.

10

51

Stevens
Point

Oneida
Indian
Reservation

41

Green Bay

De Pere

Wisconsin
Rapids

10

Appleton

Menasha

Fox R.

10

Two Rivers

Manitowoc

Black River
State Forest

Black R.

94

Petenwell
Lake

Necedah National
Wildlife Refuge

Castle Rock
Lake

Neenah

Lake
Poygan

Lake
Winnebago

Mississippi R.

53

90

90

94

39

51

Oshkosh

41

151

Fond du Lac

Kettle Moraine
State Forest

Sheboygan

43

La Crosse

14

61

Horicon National
Wildlife Refuge

41

45

Lake
Michigan

Wisconsin Dells

Baraboo

Devil's Lake
State Park

Lake
Wisconsin

Rock R.

151

West Bend

45

61

14

Wisconsin R.

12

Governor Dodge
State Park

Middleton

Sun Prairie

94

Waukesha

Milwaukee

West Allis

Kettle Moraine
State Forest

18

151

Madison

Fitchburg

39

12

18

First Capitol
State Historic Site

61

Yellowstone Lake
State Park

14

Lake
Koshkonong

43

94

Racine

360

Monroe

Janesville

Kenosha

151

Beloit

14

12

Legend

- **Interstate**
- **Major Highway**
- **City or Town**
- **State Capital**
- **Highest Point in State**
- **Historic Site**
- **National Forest**
- **State Forest**
- **National Park**
- **State Park**
- **National Wildlife Refuge**
- **Other Points of Interest**

N
W — E
S

0   miles   50

WISCONSIN ★ ★ ★ ★
MAP SKILLS

1. What is Wisconsin's northernmost national park?

2. Which major highway runs north-south through the center of the state?

3. What is Wisconsin's highest point?

4. Oshkosh is on which lake?

5. Which river flows into Lake Koshkonong?

6. Which interstate would you take from Green Bay to Milwaukee?

7. What point of interest is located near Menomonie?

8. Lake Chippewa is near which Reservation?

9. What is the northernmost island on the Door Peninsula?

10. Which town is just north of Devil's Lake State Park?

Green Bay

Geneva Lake

Wisconsin River

10. Baraboo
9. Washington Island
8. Lac Courte Oreilles Indian Reservation
7. Crystal Cave
6. Interstate 43
5. Rock River
4. Lake Winnebago
3. Timms Hill
2. Highway 51
1. Apostle Islands National Seashore

State Seal, Flag, and Song

The state seal shows the Wisconsin coat of arms along with the words "Great Seal of the State of Wisconsin." A curved line of 13 stars lies below the coat of arms. It represents the thirteen original states. The seal is round and has a sawtooth edge.

The state flag has a blue background with the state coat of arms in the center. Above the coat of arms is the state's name, and below it, the year of statehood. The coat of arms shows a large shield held by a sailor and a miner, who represent labor on water and on land. The shield bears symbols that stand for agriculture, mining, manufacturing, and shipping. To show loyalty to the country, the middle of the shield has the U.S. coat of arms. Below the shield are a horn of plenty and a pyramid of thirteen pieces of lead. The horn of plenty represents prosperity and abundance. The pyramid stands for mineral wealth and also for the thirteen original states. Above the shield is the state animal, the badger, along with a banner that carries Wisconsin's motto, "Forward."

To see the lyrics of the Wisconsin State Song, "On, Wisconsin," go to
www.statesymbolsusa.org/Wisconsin/stateSONG.html

Glossary

biologists   People who study biology, a science that deals with things that are alive (such as plants and animals).

biotechnology   The use of living cells, bacteria, etc., to make useful products (such as crops that insects are less likely to destroy or new kinds of medicine).

committee   A group of people who are chosen to do a particular job or to make decisions about something.

compensation   Something that is done or given to make up for damage, injury or suffering.

conservationists   People who work to protect animals, plants, and natural resources.

council   A group of people who are chosen to make rules, laws, or decisions about something.

endangered   In danger of no longer existing.

heritage   The traditions, achievements, beliefs, etc., that are part of the history of a group or nation.

hydropower   Electricity produced from machines that are run by moving water.

immigrants   People who come to a country to live there.

legislature   A group of people with the power to make or change laws.

migrates   Moves from one place to another.

pesticides   Chemicals that are used to kill insects that damage plants or crops.

trustees   Members of a group that manage the money of an organization.

tuition   Money that is paid to a school for the right to study there.

turbines   Engines that have parts with blades that are made to spin by pressure from water, steam, or air.

More About Wisconsin

BOOKS

Blashfield, Jean F. *Wisconsin (America the Beautiful)*. New York, NY: Children's Press, 2014.

Demuth, Patricia Brennan. *Who Was Laura Ingalls Wilder?* New York, NY: Grosset & Dunlap, 2013.

Knickelbine, Scott. *The Great Peshtigo Fire: Stories and Science from America's Deadliest Fire*. Madison, WI: Wisconsin Historical Society Press, 2012.

Nardo, Don. *Frank Lloyd Wright (Eye on Art)*. San Diego, CA: Lucent Books, 2012.

Parker, Janice. *Wisconsin: The Badger State*. New York, NY: Av2 by Weigl, 2011.

WEBSITES

State of Wisconsin:

www.wisconsin.gov

Wisconsin Department of Natural Resources: EEK! Environmental Education for Kids:

dnr.wi.gov/org/caer/ce/eek/

Wisconsin Department of Tourism:

www.travelwisconsin.com

ABOUT THE AUTHORS

Margaret Dornfeld is a writer, editor, and translator. She likes to travel to Milwaukee to visit family, explore old neighborhoods, and enjoy the city's German cuisine. Dornfeld's German ancestors settled in Lebanon, Wisconsin, around 1850.

Richard Hantula and his family come from the Gogebic Range of Wisconsin and Michigan. Now based in New York, Hantula has worked as a writer and editor for more than three decades.

Index

Page numbers in **boldface** are illustrations.

Index